SELECTED FROM

Contemporary American Plays

*Supplementary material by the staff of
Literacy Volunteers of New York City*

WRITERS' VOICES
Literacy Volunteers of New York City

SELECTED FROM CONTEMPORARY AMERICAN PLAYS was made possible by a grant from the Hale Matthews Foundation.

Selections: From THE ODD COUPLE by Neil Simon. Copyright © 1966 by Nancy Enterprises, Inc. Reprinted by permission of Random House, Inc. From *for colored girls who have considered suicide/when the rainbow is enuf* by ntozake shange. Copyright © 1975, 1976, 1977 by Ntozake Shange. Reprinted with permission of Collier Books, an imprint of Macmillan Publishing Company. From HOLD ME! by Jules Feiffer. Copyright © 1977 by Jules Feiffer. Reprinted by permission of the author. From 'NIGHT, MOTHER by Marsha Norman. Copyright © 1983 by Marsha Norman. Reprinted by permission of Hill and Wang, a division of Farrar, Straus and Giroux, Inc. From FENCES by August Wilson. Copyright © 1986 by August Wilson. Reprinted by arrangement with PLUME, an Imprint of New American Library, a Division of Penguin Books USA Inc., New York, New York. From THE TRIP TO BOUNTIFUL by Horton Foote. Copyright © 1953, 1954, 1982 by Horton Foote. Screenplay copyright © 1986, 1989 by Horton Foote. Reprinted by permission of Lucy Kroll Agency. From DRIVING MISS DAISY by Alfred Uhry. Copyright © 1986 by Alfred Uhry. Used by permission of Flora Roberts, Inc.

Supplementary materials © 1990 by Literacy Volunteers of New York City Inc.

All rights reserved. This book may not be reproduced in whole or in part, in any form or by any means, without permission.

Printed in the United States of America.

96 95 94 93 92 91 90 10 9 8 7 6 5 4 3 2 1

First LVNYC Printing: April 1990

ISBN 0-929631-15-3

Writers' Voices is a series of books published by Literacy Volunteers of New York City Inc., 121 Avenue of the Americas, New York, NY 10013. The words, "Writers' Voices," are a trademark of Literacy Volunteers of New York City.

Cover design by Paul Davis Studio; interior design by Barbara Huntley.
Publishing Director, LVNYC: Nancy McCord
Executive Director, LVNYC: Eli Zal
(The following page is an extension of the copyright page.)

CAUTION: The individual plays excerpted in SELECTED FROM CONTEMPORARY AMERICAN PLAYS are subject to a royalty. They are fully protected under the copyright laws of the United States of America, and of all countries covered by the International Copyright Union (including the Dominion of Canada and the rest of the British Commonwealth), and of all countries covered by the Pan-American Copyright Convention and the Universal Copyright Convention, and of all countries with which the United States has reciprocal copyright relations. All rights, including professional, amateur, motion picture, recitation, lecturing, public reading, radio broadcasting, television, video or sound taping, all other forms of mechanical or electronic reproduction, such as information storage and retrieval systems and photocopying, and the rights of translation into foreign languages, are strictly reserved. No part of these plays may be performed, recited, recorded or broadcast in any media without permission in writing from the authors' agents.

ACKNOWLEDGMENTS

Literacy Volunteers of New York City gratefully acknowledges the generous support and encouragement of the Hale Matthews Foundation that made the publication of this book possible.

This book could not have been realized without the kind and generous cooperation of the playwrights and their representatives: Jules Feiffer and his agent, The Lantz Office, Inc.; Horton Foote and his agent, the Lucy Kroll Agency; Marsha Norman and her publisher, Farrar, Straus & Giroux, Inc.; Ntozake Shange and her publisher, Collier Books; Neil Simon, his agent, Gary DaSilva, and his publisher, Random House, Inc.; Alfred Uhry and his agent, Flora Roberts, Inc.; and August Wilson, his publisher, New American Library, and John Berglio of Weiss, Rifkind, Wharton and Garrison.

We deeply appreciate the contributions of the following suppliers: Cam Steel Rule Die Works Inc. (steel cutting die for display); Canadian Pacific Forest Products Ltd. (text stock); Creative Graphics, Inc. (text typesetting); Horizon Paper Co., Inc. (cover stock); Martin/Friess Communications (display header); Mergenthaler Container (corrugated display); Phototype Color Graphics (cover color separations); and Ringier America Dresden Division (cover and text printing and binding).

For their guidance and assistance, we wish to thank the LVNYC Board of Directors' Publishing Committee: James E. Galton, Marvel Entertainment Group; Virginia Barber, Virginia Barber Literary Agency, Inc.; Jeff Brown; George P. Davidson, Ballantine Books; Geraldine E. Rhoads, Diamandis Communications Inc.; Virginia Rice, Reader's Digest; Martin Singerman, News America Publishing, Inc.; and Irene Yuss, Pocket Books.

Thanks also to Caron Harris and Steve Palmer of Ballantine Books for production assistance. Thanks to Jeff Brown for his editorial advice and skill, and to Sergei Boissier for proofreading.

Our thanks to Paul Davis Studio and Myrna Davis, Paul Davis, and Jeanine Esposito for their inspired design of the covers of WRITERS' VOICES. Thanks also to Barbara Huntley for her sensitive attention to the interior design of this series and to Karen Bernath for her help.

And finally, special credit must be given to Marilyn Boutwell, Jean Fargo and Gary Murphy of the LVNYC staff for their major contributions to the educational and editorial content of these books.

CONTENTS

About Writers' Voices 6

Note to the Reader 7

Introduction 11

Selected from The Odd Couple (1966),
by Neil Simon 17

Selected from for colored girls who
have considered suicide/when the
rainbow is enuf (1975),
by ntozake shange 24

Selected from Hold Me! (1977),
by Jules Feiffer 29

Selected from 'Night, Mother (1983),
by Marsha Norman 34

Selected from Fences (1986),
by August Wilson 39

Selected from The Trip to Bountiful
(1986, 1989), by Horton Foote 47

Selected from Driving Miss Daisy (1987),
by Alfred Uhry 58

ABOUT *WRITERS' VOICES*

"I want to read what others do—what I see people reading in libraries, on the subway, and at home."
Mamie Moore, a literacy student,
Brooklyn, New York

Writers' Voices is our response to Mamie Moore's wish:
- the wish to step forward into the reading community,
- the wish to have access to new information,
- the wish to read to her grandchildren,
- the wish to read for the joy of reading.

NOTE TO THE READER

"What we are familiar with, we cease to see. The writer shakes up the familiar scene, and, as if by magic, we see a new meaning in it."   Anaïs Nin

Writers' Voices invites you to discover new meaning. One way to discover new meaning is to learn something new. Another is to see in a new way something you already know.

Writers' Voices is a series of books. Each book contains selections from one or more writer's work. We chose the selections because the writers' voices can be clearly heard. Also, they deal with experiences that are interesting to think about and discuss.

If you are a new reader, you may want to have a selection read aloud to you, perhaps more than once. This will free you to enjoy the piece, to hear the language used, and to think about its meaning. Even if you are a more experienced reader, you may enjoy hearing the selection read aloud before reading it silently to yourself.

We encourage you to read *actively*. An active reader does many things—while reading, and before and after reading—that help him or her better understand and enjoy a book. Here are some suggestions of things you can do:

BEFORE READING

• Read the front and back covers of the book, and look at the cover illustration. Ask yourself what you expect the book to be about, based on this information.

• Think about why you want to read this book. What do you want to discover, and what questions do you hope will be answered?

• Look at the contents page. Decide which selections you want to read and in what order you want to read them.

DURING READING

• Try to stay with the flow of the language. If you find any words or sentences you don't understand, keep reading to see if the meaning becomes clear. If it doesn't, go back and reread the difficult part or discuss it with others.

• Try to put yourself into the play.

• Ask yourself questions as you read. For example: Do I believe this play or this character? Why?

AFTER READING

• Ask yourself if the play makes you see any of your own experiences in a new way.

• Ask yourself if the play has given you any new information.

• Keep a journal in which you can write down your thoughts about what you have read and save new words you have learned.

- Talk about what you have read with others.

Good writing should make you think after you put a book down. Whether you are a beginning reader, a more experienced reader, or a teacher of reading, we encourage you to take time to think about this book and to discuss your thoughts with others. If you want to read more plays by the authors of the selections, you can go to your bookstore or library to find them.

When you are finished with this book, we hope you will write to our editors about your reactions. We want to know your thoughts about this book and what it has meant to you.

INTRODUCTION

Plays are written to be seen and heard. This is what makes playwriting different from other kinds of writing. A playwright writes a play with the hope that it will be acted on a stage before an audience.

Plays are mostly dialogue. They tell their story and make their points through the spoken word. You also learn about the story from the actors' movements and expressions. And you pick up more information from the stage setting.

SEEING A PLAY

When you see a play, you hear the playwright's words spoken. But the producers and the director have determined what you see.

The set has been created by the scene designer. The lighting designer has created a mood.

The play has been cast and that defines

the characters' basic look. The costume designer has dressed the actors. And a make-up artist may have changed the actors' appearances. The actors speak the way they and the director think is right for each character. They move as they and the director think best.

READING A PLAY

But plays are also meant to be read. Reading a play is very different from seeing a play. When you read a play, **you** must make the play come alive.

You think about how the playwright imagined the play to look and sound. Because you read character and setting descriptions and the stage directions, you know what the playwright wanted the director to know. You also know what the playwright wanted the actors to know. From there on, it is up to you and your imagination.

You must imagine how the characters look—how tall they are, what color hair they have, how they are dressed. Even though playwrights describe the characters, they usually don't tell you everything about them.

You must imagine if the characters are shouting or whispering, if they are joking or crying, or even if they have an accent of some kind. Even though playwrights sometimes give directions on how a character should speak, they don't do this all the time.

You must imagine what the characters are doing. Even though playwrights tell when their characters enter and exit the stage, they usually don't describe every move they make.

When you read a play, you become the producer, the director, and the actors. You take the playwright's words and make your own version of the play.

HOW TO READ A PLAY

Plays look different from other kinds of writing when you see them on the printed page. Dialogue that is meant to be said aloud to the audience is set in one kind of type. Stage directions and other information for the actors and the director are set in another kind of type. One means "say this." The other means "do this."

Whenever a character is supposed to speak, the character's name appears in capital letters. The words he or she is supposed to say follow the name.

HOW TO READ THIS BOOK

The selections in this book show you how different playwrights write. While reading a play, you get to hear the playwright's voice. In each of the selections, you will hear the playwright's voice in the words the characters speak. And you will also hear the playwright's voice through the story each has chosen to tell and the way it is told. Some have chosen comedy; some have chosen tragedy; some have chosen a dramatic story.

In some plays, you will find detailed stage directions. In others, you will find detailed character descriptions. These will show you how a playwright tells the director and the actors what he or she thinks is important.

Our introductions to the plays point out qualities that are special about each play and what may be unusual in the selection.

Begin your reading with the introduction to each selected play. Also read any descriptions or directions the playwright has given. Think what you know about the play before you begin reading the dialogue. Try to make a picture in your mind of the characters. Imagine how they might sound. Think of how the setting might look. This will help as you read the selection.

You might also want to read the lines aloud, as if you were an actor. You could experiment with saying the lines in different ways—angrily, sadly, or jokingly, for example. You might even read the play with one or more people. You could each take a different part.

Selected from Contemporary American Plays is meant to introduce you to the joys of reading plays. We hope it will inspire you to study more about the craft of playwriting and to write your own play.

This book is the first of three books on plays that we are publishing. The second book will discuss how to write a play. The third book will present plays written by you, our readers. We hope you will send us your play to consider for this future book. Please send it to the editors at our address, which is in the front of the book.

SELECTED FROM
THE ODD COUPLE
by Neil Simon

EDITORS' INTRODUCTION

The Odd Couple is a comedy written by Neil Simon. It later was the basis for a successful television show.

In his plays, Neil Simon's characters show the humor in their everyday actions and feelings. We are meant to identify with his characters as we laugh at them.

The Odd Couple takes place in New York City in the present time. Oscar Madison is divorced and lives alone in a large apartment. When his friend, Felix Ungar, shows up at their weekly poker game and announces that his wife has thrown him out, Oscar says Felix can stay with him.

Even though Oscar and Felix are best friends, they have very different habits. Oscar is messy and Felix is neat. After two weeks in the same apartment, the two men are at each other's throats.

In his stage directions, Neil Simon shows the humor in the situation and points up the contrast between the two men. The selection is the beginning of the third act, which is the last act of the play.

SELECTED FROM
THE ODD COUPLE

The next evening about 7:30 P.M. The room is once again set up for the poker game, with the dining table pulled down, the chairs set about it, and the love seat moved back beneath the windows in the alcove. FELIX appears from the bedroom with a vacuum cleaner. He is doing a thorough job on the rug. As he vacuums around the table, the door opens and OSCAR comes in wearing a summer hat and carrying a newspaper. He glares at FELIX, who is still vacuuming, and shakes his head contemptuously. He crosses behind FELIX, leaving his hat on the side table next to the armchair, and goes into his bedroom. FELIX is not aware of his presence. Then suddenly the power stops on the vacuum, as OSCAR has obviously pulled the plug in the bedroom. FELIX tries switching the button on and off a few times, then turns to go back into the bedroom. He stops and realizes what's happened as OSCAR comes back into the room. OSCAR takes a cigar out of his pocket and as he crosses in front of FELIX to the couch, he unwraps it and drops the wrappings carelessly on the floor. He then steps up on the couch and walks back and forth mashing down the pillows. Stepping down, he plants one foot on the armchair and then sits on the couch, taking a wooden match from the coffee table and striking it on the table to light his cigar. He flips the used match onto the rug and settles back to read his newspaper. FELIX has watched this all in silence, and now carefully picks up the cigar wrappings and the match and drops them into OSCAR's hat. He then dusts his hands and takes the vacuum cleaner into the kitchen, pulling the cord in after him. OSCAR takes the wrappings from the hat and puts them in the butt-filled ashtray on the coffee table. Then he takes the ashtray and dumps it on the floor. As he once more settles down with his newspaper, FELIX comes out of the kitchen carrying a tray with a steaming dish of spaghetti. As he crosses behind OSCAR to the table, he indicates that it smells delicious and passes it close to OSCAR to make sure OSCAR smells the fantastic dish he's missing. As FELIX sits and begins to eat, OSCAR takes a can of aerosol spray from the bar, and circling the table, sprays all around FELIX, then puts the can down next to him and goes back to his newspaper.

FELIX: [Pushing the spaghetti away] All right, how much longer is this gonna go on?

OSCAR: [Reading his paper] Are you talking to me?

FELIX: That's right, I'm talking to you.

OSCAR: What do you want to know?

FELIX: I want to know if you're going to spend the rest of your life not talking to me. Because if you are, I'm going to buy a radio. [No reply] Well? [No reply] I see. You're not going to talk to me. [No reply] All right. Two can play at this game. [Pause] If you're not going to talk to me, I'm not going to talk to you. [No reply]

I can act childish too, you know. [*No reply*] I can go on without talking just as long as you can.

OSCAR: Then why the hell don't you shut up?

FELIX: Are you talking to me?

OSCAR: You had your chance to talk last night. I begged you to come upstairs with me. From now on I never want to hear a word from that shampooed head as long as you live. That's a warning, Felix.

FELIX: [*Stares at him*] I stand warned. Over and out!

OSCAR: [*Gets up, takes a key out of his pocket and slams it on the table*] There's a key to the back door. If you stick to the hallway and your room, you won't get hurt.

[*He sits back down on the couch*]

FELIX: I don't think I gather the entire meaning of that remark.

OSCAR: Then I'll explain it to you. Stay out of my way.

FELIX: [*Picks up the key and moves to the couch*] I think you're serious. I think you're really serious. Are you serious?

OSCAR: This is my apartment. Everything in my apartment is mine. The only thing here that's yours is you. Just stay in your room and speak softly.

FELIX: Yeah, you're serious. Well, let me remind you that I pay half the rent and I'll go into any room I want.
[*He gets up angrily and starts toward the hallway*]

OSCAR: Where are you going?

FELIX: I'm going to walk around your bedroom.

OSCAR: [*Slams down his newspaper*] You stay out of there.

FELIX: [*Steaming*] Don't tell me where to go. I pay a hundred and twenty dollars a month.

OSCAR: That was off-season. Starting tomorrow the rates are twelve dollars a day.

FELIX: All right. [*He takes some bills out of his pocket and slams them down on the table*] There you are. I'm paid up for today. Now I'm going to walk in your bedroom.

[*He starts to storm off*]

OSCAR: Stay out of there! Stay out of my room!

[*He chases after him.* FELIX *dodges around the table as* OSCAR *blocks the hallway*]

FELIX: [*Backing away, keeping the table between them*] Watch yourself! Just watch yourself, Oscar!

OSCAR: [*With a pointing finger*] I'm warning you. You want to live here, I don't want to see you, I don't want to hear you and I don't want to smell your cooking. Now get this spaghetti off my poker table.

FELIX: Ha! Ha, ha!

OSCAR: What the hell's so funny?

FELIX: It's not spaghetti. It's linguini!

[OSCAR *picks up the plate of linguini, crosses to the doorway and hurls it into the kitchen*]

OSCAR: Now it's garbage!

SELECTED FROM
for colored girls who have considered suicide/when the rainbow is enuf
by ntozake shange

EDITORS' INTRODUCTION

For colored girls who have considered suicide/when the rainbow is enuf *was written by ntozake shange. Shange calls her play a "choreopoem." She wrote the play as a poem with music, song, and dance.*

The play has seven characters, all black women. Each character wears a different color dress and that is how they are identified. Together they are meant to stand for all black women.

The women tell of their lives. They talk and sing about their relationships with men. And they talk and sing about their struggles to find and keep their own identities.

Shange, who is also a poet, chose to write her play in a special way. She used no capital letters, not even for her own name. She spelled words the way they sound, not the *way they are really spelled. She used punctuation only when absolutely necessary.*

The play takes place in the present. It is acted on a bare stage, and there is only one act. The characters speak to one another and to the audience. They each tell their own story in poetry.

SELECTED FROM for colored girls who have considered suicide/ when the rainbow is enuf

LADY IN BLUE: that niggah will be back tomorrow, sayin 'i'm sorry'

LADY IN YELLOW: get this, last week my old man came in saying, 'i don't know how she got yr number baby, i'm sorry.'

LADY IN BROWN: no this one is it, 'o baby, ya know i waz high, i'm sorry'

LADY IN PURPLE: 'i'm only human, and inadequacy is what makes us human, & if we was perfect we wdnt have nothin to strive for, so you might as well go on and forgive me pretty baby, cause i'm sorry'

LADY IN GREEN: 'shut up bitch, i told you
i waz sorry'

LADY IN ORANGE: no this one is it, 'i do ya
like i do ya cause i thot ya could take it,
now i'm sorry'

LADY IN RED: 'now i know that ya know i
love ya, but i aint ever gonna love ya
like ya want me to love ya, i'm sorry'

LADY IN BLUE: one thing i dont need
is any more apologies
i got sorry greetin me at my front door
you can keep yrs
i dont know what to do wit em
they dont open doors
or bring the sun back
they dont make me happy
or get a morning paper
didnt nobody stop using my tears to
                              wash cars

cuz a sorry
i am simply tired
of collectin
    i didnt know
    i was so important to you'
i'm gonna haveta throw some away
i cant get to the clothes in my closet

for alla the sorries
i'm gonna tack a sign to my door
leave a message by the phone
    'if you called
    to say yr sorry
    call somebody
    else
    i dont use em anymore'
i let sorry/didn't meanta/& how cd
                      i know abt that
take a walk down a dark & musty street
                          in brooklyn
i'm gonna do exactly what i want to
& i wont be sorry for none of it
letta sorry soothe yr soul/i'm gonna
                        soothe mine

you were always inconsistent
doin somethin & then bein sorry
beatin my heart to death
talkin bout you sorry
well
i will not call
i'm not going to be nice
i will raise my voice
& scream & holler
& break things & race the engine

& tell all yr secrets bout yrself to yr face
& i will list in detail everyone of my
                        wonderful lovers
& their ways
i will play oliver lake
loud
& i wont be sorry for none of it

i loved you on purpose
i was open on purpose
i still crave vulnerability & close talk
& i'm not even sorry bout you bein sorry
you can carry all the guilt & grime
                        ya wanna
just dont give it to me
i cant use another sorry
next time
you should admit
you're mean/low-down/triflin/& no
                        count straight out
steada bein sorry alla the time
enjoy bein yrself

SELECTED FROM
HOLD ME!
by Jules Feiffer

EDITORS' INTRODUCTION

Hold Me! is a comedy written by Jules Feiffer. Feiffer calls his play "an entertainment." That is because each act is made up of many short humorous scenes. Each scene stands on its own. But taken all together, they tell about the reality of human relationships in a world filled with anxiety.

The play has many different characters. Most of the characters are called by such names as "husband" or "wife." They are not meant to be a specific person—they are meant to be any person.

Many of the scenes in this play are monologues. In monologues, actors can speak directly to the audience, to another actor, to someone off stage, or to themselves. In writing a monologue, the playwright may not make paragraphs. He will let the actor break up the long thought with his voice or actions.

This play is set in the present. The stage has almost no furniture, and there are very few props.

SELECTED FROM HOLD ME!

Brands

HUSBAND: I used to read them ads—know what I mean? "Even your best friend won't tell you" ads—and it used to bother me because if you're a right guy—nice to your mother and everything—what kind of girl is it who'd throw you over because of the wrong toothpaste you used—or what kind of phoney friend is it who'd spend his time not drinking with you but smelling you? And then it would bother me how these people in the ads would become popular overnight by changing brand names. [*He rises and crosses down left to barrel and sits.*] I mean they didn't change their insides—they weren't better people. But suddenly they'd switch brands and become pride of the regiment. Well this used to bother me because, frankly, people never have taken to me. Like at the job the only desk during breaks where you can't hear a steady buzz-buzz of conversation is mine. Nobody ever comes over to me! I always got to go over to them. All my life. When I was a kid and three of us would walk down the street? I'd never be in the middle. I'd always be on the gutter side. I never got invited to join up with any clubs. I went through the entire army without once being invited to play cards. And I admit sometimes I used to wake up in the middle of the night dripping sweat—and going on and off in my head like a big neon sign was—"Bad breath, underarm odor, bad breath." I got married and my wife treated me like a janitor. The only thing she could say nice for me was that I'm good with my hands. When the other wives boasted about their husbands' talents she'd call me in to fix the sink. So at parties I'd do my famous "fixing the sink bit" and the rest of the time we were acquaintances. And more and more in the back of my head it went—"Change your soap. Change your toothpaste." But—I don't know—I always felt that I'm me for better or worse. I'm me! Then my kids who my wife says are at a sensitive age began to make insensitive cracks. So I finally gave in. I changed my brand of toothpaste, my brand of hair oil, my brand of soap and my suit style. And son of a gun, the ads were right! My wife adored me. The kids loved me. Suddenly everybody was my buddy for the first time in my life! Three weeks of it was all I could take. Then I went back to the old ways. If they prefer that brand over me the hell with them.

More Socks

HUSBAND: I go to the laundromat to do a wash. Included in the wash are 8 pairs of socks. Out of the wash come 6 pairs of socks plus 1 gray sock and 1 blue sock. A week later I go to the laundromat to do a wash. Included in the wash are 6 pairs of socks. Out of the wash comes 4 pairs of socks plus 1 black sock and 1 green sock. A week later I go to the laundromat to do a wash. Included in the wash are 4 pairs of socks. Out of the wash comes 2 pairs of socks. The other socks never show up. The next day I go to the laundromat. As an experiment I put in nothing but my last 2 pairs of socks. Out of the wash comes a body stocking. [*He opens bundle and takes out note.*] In the body stocking I find a note. The note says: "Quit trifling with the laws of nature and bring the machine more socks."

Morning I Hate

WIFE: Mornings I hate. Going on the bus to work I hate. Work I hate. Coming home from work I hate. Sometimes I think. . . . What a relief to escape all this and get married. [*She sits right center on bed.*] And then I remember . . . I am married.

SELECTED FROM
'NIGHT, MOTHER
by Marsha Norman

EDITORS' INTRODUCTION

'Night, Mother *was written by Marsha Norman. It is a play with only two characters, a mother and a daughter, and only one act. The play takes place in the mother's home in the present time.*

Jessie Cates, the daughter, is an epileptic. She is divorced and her grown son is a disappointment. Since her divorce, she has lived with her mother and cared for her.

Jessie is tired of her life and sees no hope for her future. She has decided to kill herself tonight. But first, she will tell her mother of the plan, so it won't be a shock to her. Then she will go to her bedroom, say " 'Night, Mother" as she has every night for years, lock the door, and shoot herself.

The selection includes Marsha Norman's description of her two characters which comes before the beginning of the play. The play selection is from the last part of the play. Jessie is trying to make her mother understand how she feels.

SELECTED FROM 'NIGHT, MOTHER

Characters

JESSIE CATES: Jessie is in her late thirties or early forties, pale and vaguely unsteady, physically. It is only in the last year that Jessie has gained control of her mind and body, and tonight, she is determined to hold onto that control. She wears pants and a long black sweater with deep pockets one of which contains a notepad and there may be a pencil behind her ear or a pen clipped to one of the pockets of the sweater.

As a rule, Jessie doesn't feel much like talking. Other people have rarely found her quirky sense of humor amusing. She has a peaceful energy on this night, a sense of purpose, but is clearly aware of the time passing moment by moment. Oddly enough, Jessie has never been as communicative or as enjoyable as she is on this evening, but we must know she has not always been this way. There is a familiarity between these two women that comes from having lived together for a long time. There is a shorthand to the talk and a sense of routine comfort to the way they relate to each other physically. Naturally, there are also routine aggravations.

THELMA CATES: Thelma is Jessie's mother, in her late fifties or early sixties. She has begun to feel her age and so takes it easy when she can, or when it serves her purposes to let someone help her. But she speaks quickly and enjoys talking. She believes that things *are* what she says they are. Her sturdiness is more a mental quality than a physical one, finally. She is chatty and nosy and this is *her* house.

* * *

MAMA: How can I let you go?

JESSIE: You can because you have to. It's what you've always done.

MAMA: You are my child!

JESSIE: I am what became of your child. [*Mama cannot answer.*] I found an old baby picture of me. And it was somebody else, not me. It was somebody pink and fat who never heard of sick or lonely, somebody who cried and got fed, and reached up and got held and kicked but didn't hurt anybody, and slept whenever she wanted to, just by closing her eyes. Somebody who mainly just laid there and laughed at the colors waving around over her head and chewed on a polka-dot whale and woke up knowing some new trick nearly every day and rolled over and drooled on the sheet and felt your hand pulling my quilt back up over me. That's who I started out and this is who is left. [*There is no self-pity here.*] That's what this is about. It's somebody I lost, all right, it's my own self. Who I never was. Or who I tried to be and never got there. Somebody I waited for who never came. And never will. So, see, it doesn't much matter what else happens in the world or in this house, even. I'm what was worth waiting for and I didn't make it. Me . . . who might have made a difference to me . . . I'm not going to show up, so there's no reason to stay, except to keep you company, and that's . . . not reason enough because I'm not . . . very good company. [*A pause.*] Am I.

MAMA: [*Knowing she must tell the truth.*] No. And neither am I.

JESSIE: I had this strange little thought, well, maybe it's not so strange. Anyway, after Christmas, after I decided to do this, I would wonder, sometimes, what might keep me here, what might be worth staying for, and you know what it was? It was maybe if there was something I really liked, like maybe if I really liked rice pudding or cornflakes for breakfast or something, that might be enough.

MAMA: Rice pudding is good.

JESSIE: Not to me.

SELECTED FROM
FENCES
by August Wilson

EDITORS' INTRODUCTION

Fences was written by August Wilson. The play takes place in the front yard of Troy Maxson's house in a big American city. The play begins in 1957 and ends in 1965.

Troy was the son of a sharecropper. He came north at age 14 to find work. Being young and black, he found it hard to find a job, so he started stealing.

After a few years, Troy married and had a son, Cory. But he kept on stealing. During a robbery, he accidentally killed a man. He went to jail for 15 years.

In prison, Troy learned to play baseball. When he got out, he had a dream of playing professional ball, but he didn't make it. His wife said it was because he was too old. Troy thinks the reason was because he was black. Troy now has a steady job and has changed his life.

Troy's son, Cory, is a now a teenager. He is a good athlete and student. He has a chance to go to college on a football scholar-

ship. But Troy is afraid that white people will hurt his son, as he has been hurt.

The selection comes from the third scene in the first act.

SELECTED FROM FENCES

TROY: Your mama tell me you done got recruited by a college football team? Is that right?

CORY: Yeah. Coach Zellman say the recruiter gonna be coming by to talk to you. Get you to sign the permission papers.

TROY: I thought you supposed to be working down there at the A&P. Ain't you suppose to be working down there after school?

CORY: Mr. Stawicki say he gonna hold my job for me until after the football season. Say starting next week I can work weekends.

TROY: I thought we had an understanding about this football stuff? You suppose to keep up with your chores and hold that job down at the A&P. Ain't been around here all day on a Saturday. Ain't none of your chores done . . . and now you telling me you done quit your job.

CORY: I'm gonna be working weekends.

TROY: You damn right you are! And ain't no need for nobody coming around here to talk to me about signing nothing.

CORY: Hey, Pop . . . you can't do that. He's coming all the way from North Carolina.

TROY: I don't care where he coming from. The white man ain't gonna let you get nowhere with that football noway. You go on and get your book-learning so you can work yourself up in that A&P or learn how to fix cars or build houses or something, get you a trade. That way you have something can't nobody take away from you. You go on and learn how to put your hands to some good use. Besides hauling people's garbage.

CORY: I get good grades, Pop. That's why the recruiter wants to talk with you. You got to keep up your grades to get recruited. This way I'll be going to college. I'll get a chance . . .

TROY: First you gonna get your butt down there to the A&P and get your job back.

CORY: Mr. Stawicki done already hired somebody else 'cause I told him I was playing football.

TROY: You a bigger fool than I thought . . . to let somebody take away your job so you can play some football. Where you gonna get your money to take out your girlfriend and whatnot? What kind of foolishness is that to let somebody take away your job?

CORY: I'm still gonna be working weekends.

TROY: Naw . . . naw. You getting your butt out of here and finding you another job.

CORY: Come on, Pop! I got to practice. I can't work after school and play football too. The team needs me. That's what Coach Zellman say . . .

TROY: I don't care what nobody else say. I'm the boss . . . you understand? I'm the boss around here. I do the only saying what counts.

CORY: Come on, Pop!

TROY: I asked you . . . did you understand?

CORY: Yeah . . .

TROY: What?!

CORY: Yessir.

TROY: You go on down there to that A&P and see if you can get your job back. If you can't do both . . . then you quit the football team. You've got to take the crookeds with the straights.

CORY: Yessir.
 [*Pause.*]
Can I ask you a question?

TROY: What the hell you wanna ask me? Mr. Stawicki the one you got the questions for.

CORY: How come you ain't never liked me?

TROY: Liked you? Who the hell say I got to like you? What law is there say I got to like you? Wanna stand up in my face and ask a damn fool-ass question like that. Talking about liking somebody. Come here, boy, when I talk to you.

[CORY *comes over to where* TROY *is working. He stands slouched over and* TROY *shoves him on his shoulder.*]

Straighten up, goddammit! I asked you a question . . . what law is there say I got to like you?

CORY: None.

TROY: Well, alright then! Don't you eat every day?

[*Pause.*]

Answer me when I talk to you! Don't you eat every day?

CORY: Yeah.

TROY: Nigger, as long as you in my house, you put that sir on the end of it when you talk to me!

CORY: Yes . . . sir.

TROY: You eat every day.

CORY: Yessir!

TROY: Got a roof over your head.

CORY: Yessir!

TROY: Got clothes on your back.

CORY: Yessir.

TROY: Why you think that is?

CORY: Cause of you.

TROY: Aw, hell I know it's 'cause of me . . . but why do you think that is?

CORY: [*Hesitant.*] Cause you like me.

TROY: Like you? I go out of here every morning . . . bust my butt . . . putting up with them crackers every day . . . cause I like you? You about the biggest fool I ever saw.

[*Pause.*]

It's my job. It's my responsibility! You understand that? A man got to take care of his family. You live in my house . . . sleep you behind on my bedclothes . . . fill you belly up with my food . . . cause you my son. You my flesh and blood. Not 'cause I like you! Cause it's my duty to take care of you. I owe a responsibility to you! Let's get this straight right here . . . before it go along any further . . . I ain't got to like you. Mr. Rand don't give me my money come payday cause he likes me. He gives me cause he owe me. I done give you everything I had to give you. I gave you your life! Me and your mama worked that out between us. And liking your black ass wasn't part of the bargain. Don't you try and go through life worrying about if somebody like you or not. You best be making sure they doing right by you. You understand what I'm saying, boy?

CORY: Yessir.

TROY: Then get the hell out of my face, and get on down to that A&P.

SELECTED FROM
THE TRIP TO BOUNTIFUL
by Horton Foote

EDITORS' INTRODUCTION

The Trip to Bountiful *was originally written by Horton Foote as a play for the stage. Over thirty years later, he rewrote it as a screenplay.*

A script written for television or the movies is different from one to be performed on a stage. Because the action is not confined to a stage, the playwright can make use of different locations to help tell the story. And because the final movie will be edited from many rolls of film shot in different places and from different angles, he can use "quick cuts" to give the audience information. These cuts might be used to make us see things from different points of view. Or they might be used to show the passage of time. That is why you will find directions for the cameraman and film editor such as "interior" and "exterior."

Another difference is that the audience sees the play through the camera's eye. The camera can focus on one character or one de-

tail of the setting at a time. This lets the playwright make more use of an actor's face to describe the character's emotions. The character doesn't always need words to let the audience know how he or she is feeling.

The selection contains scenes inside and outside a bus carrying Mrs. Watts to Bountiful, Texas. Mrs. Watts was born and raised on a farm in Bountiful. After her husband died, she raised her son, Ludie, on the same farm. But the land gave out. Mrs. Watts and Ludie moved to Houston, Texas where he could find work. There Ludie met and married Jessie Mae. The three live together in a small apartment. Mrs. Watts wants to return to Bountiful before she dies. But Jessie Mae thinks she is foolish and too old and sick to go. While Ludie is at work and Jessie Mae is out, Mrs. Watts sneaks away to the bus station. She meets Thelma in the waiting room.

SELECTED FROM
THE TRIP TO BOUNTIFUL

Interior: Bus

MRS. WATTS and THELMA are seated next to each other. MRS. WATTS is by the window.

MRS. WATTS: The bus is nice to ride, isn't it?

THELMA: It is.

MRS. WATTS: Excuse me for getting personal, but what's a pretty girl like you doing traveling alone?

THELMA: My husband has just been sent overseas. I'm going to stay with my family.

MRS. WATTS: I'm sorry to hear that. Well, you just say the Ninety-first Psalm over and over to yourself. It will be a bower of strength and protection for him. "He that dwelleth in the secret place of the most high shall abide under the shadow of the Almighty. I will say of my Lord, He is my refuge and my fortress . . ."

[THELMA *is crying.* MRS. WATTS *looks up and sees her.*]

I'm sorry, honey.

THELMA: I'm just lonesome for him, that's all.

MRS. WATTS: You keep him under the Lord's wing, and he'll be safe.

THELMA: Yes Ma'am. I'm sorry. I don't know what gets into me.

MRS. WATTS: Nobody needs to be ashamed of crying. We've all dampened our pillows sometime or other. I know I have.

THELMA: If I could only learn not to worry.

MRS. WATTS: I guess we all have wished that. Jessie Mae, my daughter-in-law, don't worry. "What for?" she says. Well, like I tell her, that's a fine attitude if you can cultivate it. Trouble is, I can't any longer.

THELMA: It is hard.

MRS. WATTS: I didn't used to worry. When I was a girl I was so carefree. Had lots to worry me, too. Everybody was so poor back in Bountiful. But we got along. I said to Papa once after our third crop failure in a row . . . whoever gave this place the name Bountiful? Said his papa did. Because in those days it was a land of plenty. You just had to drop seeds in the ground and the crops would spring up. We had cotton and corn and sugar cane.

I still think it's the prettiest place I ever heard of. Jessie Mae says it's the ugliest. But she says that to bother me. She only saw it once, and then a rainy day at that. She says it's nothing but an old swamp. That may be, I said, but it's a mighty pretty swamp to me.

Exterior: Bus

The bus goes through the Texas countryside.

Interior: Bus

THELMA is reading the movie magazine, MRS. WATTS her Bible. THELMA puts her magazine down.

THELMA: Mrs. Watts?

MRS. WATTS: Yes.

THELMA: I think I ought to tell you this. I . . . I don't want you to think I'm interfering in your business, but well, you see, your son and your daughter-in-law came in just after you left . . .

MRS. WATTS: Oh, I know. I saw them coming. That's why I left so fast.

THELMA: Your son seemed very concerned.

MRS. WATTS: Bless his heart.

THELMA: He found a handkerchief that you had dropped.

MRS. WATTS: That's right. I did.

THELMA: He asked me if I had seen you. I felt I had to say yes. I wouldn't have said anything if he hadn't asked me.

MRS. WATTS: Oh, that's all right. I would have done the same thing in your place. Did you talk to Jessie Mae?

THELMA: Yes.

MRS. WATTS: Isn't she a sight? I bet she told you I was crazy.

THELMA: Well . . .

MRS. WATTS: No. You needn't worry about it hurting my feelings. Poor Jessie Mae, she thinks everybody's crazy that don't want to sit in the beauty parlor all day and drink Coca-Colas. You know, I think Ludie knows how I feel about getting back to Bountiful, because once when we were talkin' about something we did back there in the old days, he burst out crying. He was so overcome he had to leave the room.

Exterior: Bus

The bus continues through the Texas countryside.

Interior: Bus

THELMA *has her eyes closed.* MRS. WATTS *is looking out the window and humming.*

THELMA: That's a pretty hymn. What's the name of that?

MRS. WATTS: "There's Not a Friend Like the Lovely Jesus." Do you like hymns?

THELMA: Yes, I do.

MRS. WATTS: So do I. Jessie Mae says they've gone out of style, but I don't agree. What's your favorite hymn?

THELMA: I don't know.

MRS. WATTS: The one I was singing is mine. I bet I sing it a hundred times a day. When Jessie Mae isn't home. Hymns make Jessie Mae nervous. Jessie Mae hates me. I don't know why, but she hates me. Hate me or not, I gotta get back and smell that salt air and work that dirt. Callie said I could always come back and visit her and she meant it too. That's who I'm going to stay with now. Callie Davis. The whole first month of my visit I am going to work in Callie's garden. I haven't had my hands in dirt in twenty years. My hands feel the need of dirt. Do you like to work the land?

THELMA: I never have.

MRS. WATTS: Try it sometime. It'll do wonders for you. I bet I'll live to be a hundred. If I could just get outdoors. It was being cooped up in those two rooms that was killing me. I used to work the land like a man. Had to when Papa died. I got two little babies buried there. Renee Sue and Douglas. Diphtheria got Renee Sue. I never knew what carried Douglas away. He was just weak from the start. I know that Callie's kept up their graves. Oh, if my heart just holds out until I get there. Now, where do you go after Harrison?

THELMA: Old Gulf. My family have just moved there from Louisiana. I'll stay there with them until my husband comes home again.

MRS. WATTS: That's nice.

THELMA: It'll be funny living at home again.

MRS. WATTS: How long have you been married?

THELMA: A year. My husband was anxious for me to go. He said he'd worry about my being alone. I'm the only child and my parents and I are very close.

MRS. WATTS: That's nice.

THELMA: I so hoped my mother and daddy would like my husband and he'd like them. I needn't have worried. They hit it off from the very first. Mother and Daddy say they feel like they have two children now. A son and a daughter.

MRS. WATTS: Isn't that nice. I've heard people say that when your son marries you lose a son, but when your daughter marries you get a son. What's your husband's name?

THELMA: Robert.

MRS. WATTS: That's a nice name.

THELMA: I think so. I guess any name he had I would think was nice. I love my husband very much. Lots of girls I know think I'm silly about him, but I can't help it.

MRS. WATTS: I wasn't in love with my husband. Do you believe we are punished for the things we do wrong? I sometimes think that's why I've had all my trouble. I've talked to many a preacher about it; all but one said they didn't think so. But I can't see any other reason. Of course, I didn't lie to my husband. I told him I didn't love him. That I admired him, which I did, but I didn't love him. That I'd never love anybody but Ray John Murray as long as I lived. And I didn't and I couldn't help it. Even when my husband died and I had to move back with Mama and Papa I used to sit on the front gallery every morning and every evening just to nod hello to Ray John Murray as he went by the house to work at the store. He went a mile out of his way to pass the house. He never loved nobody but me.

THELMA: Why didn't you marry him?

MRS. WATTS: Because his papa and my papa didn't speak. My papa forced me to write a letter saying I never wanted to see him again, and he got drunk and married out of spite. I felt sorry for his wife. She knew he never loved her. [*A pause.*] Well, I don't think about those things now. But they're all part of Bountiful. I think that's why I'm starting to think of them again. You're lucky to be married to the man you love.

THELMA: I know I am.

MRS. WATTS: Awfully lucky.

SELECTED FROM
DRIVING MISS DAISY
by Alfred Uhry

EDITORS' INTRODUCTION

Driving Miss Daisy was written by Alfred Uhry. The play has only one act, but 25 different scenes. These scenes take us from 1948 to 1973. It is set in and around Atlanta, Georgia. The scenes are set in many different places around town. Yet Uhry makes each scene flow into the next scene.

Miss Daisy is Daisy Werthan, a Jewish widow and retired school teacher. She is 72 years old when the play begins. The other characters are her grown son Boolie and Hoke Coleman, her black chauffeur. Hoke is 60 years old when the play begins.

Daisy has wrecked her car. Her son decides she needs a chauffeur. Daisy hates the idea. When Hoke comes to work for her, Daisy refuses to let him drive her. But, over time, she comes to love, trust, and respect him. And Hoke comes to love, trust, and respect her.

The selection is the ninth scene in the play.

SELECTED FROM
DRIVING MISS DAISY

June 1950

We hear sounds of birds twittering. Lights come up brightly—hot sun. DAISY, *in light dress, is kneeling, a trowel in hand, working by a gravestone.* HOKE, *jacket in hand, sleeves rolled up, stands nearby.*

HOKE: I jess thinkin', Miz Daisy. We been out heah to the cemetery three times dis mont already and ain' even the twentieth yet.

DAISY: It's good to come in nice weather.

HOKE: Yassum. Mist' Sig's grave mighty well tended. I b'lieve you the best widow in the state of Georgia.

DAISY: Boolie's always pestering me to let the staff out here tend to this grave. Perpetual care, they call it.

HOKE: Doan you do it. It right to have somebody from the family lookin' after you.

DAISY: I'll certainly never have that. Boolie will have me in perpetual care before I'm cold.

HOKE: Come on now, Miz Daisy.

DAISY: Hoke, run back to the car and get that pot of azaleas for me and set it on Leo Bauer's grave.

HOKE: Miz Rose Bauer's husband?

DAISY: That's right. She asked me to bring it out here for her. She's not very good about coming. And I believe today would've been Leo's birthday.

HOKE: Yassum. Where the grave at?

DAISY: I'm not exactly sure. But I know it's over that way on the other side of the weeping cherry. You'll see the headstone. Bauer.

HOKE: Yassum.

DAISY: What's the matter?

HOKE: Nothin' the matter.

[HE *exits.* SHE *works with her trowel. In a moment* HOKE *returns with flowers*]

Miz Daisy . . .

DAISY: I told you it's over on the other side of the weeping cherry. It says Bauer on the headstone.

HOKE: How'd that look?

DAISY: What are you talking about?

HOKE: [*Deeply embarrassed*] I'm talkin' bout I cain read.

DAISY: What?

HOKE: I cain read.

DAISY: That's ridiculous. Anybody can read.

HOKE: Nome. Not me.

DAISY: Then how come I see you looking at the paper all the time?

HOKE: That's it. Jes' lookin. I dope out what's happening from the pictures.

DAISY: You know your letters, don't you?

HOKE: My ABC's? Yassum, pretty good. I jes' cain read.

DAISY: Stop saying that. It's making me mad. If you know your letters then you can read. You just don't know you can read.

I taught some of the stupidest children God ever put on the face of this earth and all of them could read enough to find a name on a tombstone. The name is Bauer. Buh buh buh buh Bauer. What letter sounds like buh?

HOKE: Sounds like a B.

DAISY: Of course. Buh Bauer. Er er er er er. BauER. That's the last part. What letter sounds like er?

HOKE: R?

DAISY: So the first letter is a—

HOKE: B.

DAISY: And the last letter is an—

HOKE: R.

DAISY: B-R. B-R. B-R. Brr. Brr. Brr. It even sounds like Bauer, doesn't it?

HOKE: Sho' do, Miz Daisy.

DAISY: That's it. Now go over there like I told you in the first place and look for a headstone with a B at the beginning and an R at the end and that will be Bauer.

HOKE: We ain' gon' worry 'bout what come in the middle?

DAISY: Not right now. This will be enough for you to find it. Go on now.

HOKE: Yassum.

DAISY: And don't come back here telling me you can't do it. You can.

HOKE: Miz Daisy . . .

DAISY: What now?

HOKE: I 'preciate this, Miz Daisy.

DAISY: Don't be ridiculous! I didn't do anything. Now would you please hurry up? I'm burning up out here.

WRITERS' VOICES

Kareem Abdul-Jabbar and Peter Knobler, *Selected from GIANT STEPS*, $3.50

Rudolfo A. Anaya, *Selected from BLESS ME, ULTIMA*, $3.50

Maya Angelou, *Selected from I KNOW WHY THE CAGED BIRD SINGS and THE HEART OF A WOMAN*, $3.50

Peter Benchley, *Selected from JAWS*, $3.50

Carol Burnett, *Selected from ONE MORE TIME*, $3.50

Mary Higgins Clark, *Selected from THE LOST ANGEL*, $3.50

Avery Corman, *Selected from KRAMER VS. KRAMER*, $3.50

Bill Cosby, *Selected from FATHERHOOD and TIME FLIES*, $3.50

Louise Erdrich, *Selected from LOVE MEDICINE*, $3.50

Maxine Hong Kingston, *Selected from CHINA MEN and THE WOMAN WARRIOR*, $3.50

Loretta Lynn with George Vecsey, *Selected from COAL MINER'S DAUGHTER*, $3.50

Selected from CONTEMPORARY AMERICAN PLAYS, $3.50

To order, please send your check to Publishing Program, Literacy Volunteers of New York City, 121 Avenue of the Americas, New York, NY 10013. Please add $1.50 per order and .50 per book to cover postage and handling. NY and NJ residents, add appropriate sales tax. Prices subject to change without notice.